# DIVINE FEMININE
## THE SPIRITUAL AWAKENING OF THE SOUL
# BALANCED

CAREY HARRIS

**DIVINE FEMININE:**
**THE SPRITUAL AWAKEING OF THE SOUL BALANCED**

Copyright © 2018 by Carey Harris.

All Rights Reserved. No part of this publication may be reproduced, distributed, or transmitted in any form or by any means, including photocopying, recording, or other electronic or mechanical methods, or by any information storage and retrieval system without the prior written permission of the publisher, except in the case of very brief quotations embodied in critical reviews and certain other noncommercial uses permitted by copyright law.

For information contact:
Tausha Matt, 620 W Mc Carthy Way 60, Los Angeles, CA 90089, Email: info@snhpr.com

First Printing: Aug 2018

ISBN: 978-1-7325543-0-6

# TABLE OF CONTENTS

INTRODUCTION ............................................................ 5

CHAPTER 1 .................................................................... 7

THE MISUNDERSTANDING

CHAPTER 2 .................................................................. 11

THE ALCHEMICAL YOU

CHAPTER 3 .................................................................. 15

STORIES OF THE FEMININE DIVINE

    Divine feminine: Bringing back the essence ............................................................ 22

    Divine feminine: The manifestation of the feminine principle ................................... 23

    The divine feminine: The interplay of the feminine and masculine principles ............ 24

Divine feminine: It exists within all of us .................. 25

## CHAPTER 4 ............................................................ 27
## WHOLE BRAIN THINKING

Whole Brain Thinking - Honoring the Divine Feminine ............................................. 28

What is Whole Braining Thinking? ............ 29

What is the Divine Feminine Way to God? ............................................................ 30

What Does the Divine Feminine Value? .... 31

Moving Into Whole Brain Thinking ........... 32

## CHAPTER 5 ............................................................ 39
## THE RETURN OF THE FEMININE

## CHAPTER 6 ............................................................ 45
## FEMININE POWER

## CHAPTER 7 ............................................................ 53
## SURRENDERING TO DIVINE FEMININE

# INTRODUCTION

The divine feminine shows the existence of the mother within us all and the universe. It is upon us rite now in the form of thoughts, dreams, images and symbols. It also represents fertility, reproduction, movement, creativity and generation. The energy in this form is the mystery as well as the reality of the universe and symbolizes the existence of the supreme as the source of all life. If we look from the ancient times to current day we find that the divine feminine is related to the process of death, destruction, decay, rebirth, purification, transformation and illumination of matter. The divine feminine archetypes portray the truth of life in the fullest of forms.

The meeting of the spiritual and the material world is only possible through the manifestation of the divine feminine. This truth of divine feminine and its manifestations has to be reemphasized in today's world which has all but forgotten the real nature of the universe and the supreme.

# CHAPTER 1

# THE MISUNDERSTANDING

I am not that interested in someone's gender. I am interested in their wholeness. Just because someone identifies as female doesn't mean they are working on behalf of the "Divine Feminine".

If more females are moving into positions of so-called power but they are operating on the patriarchal mindset, then it's hardly progress. It's only adding to the illusions and confusion around what power and equality really mean.

The term patriarchy can trigger judgements that anyone with a penis is patriarchal. The patriarchal mindset is not gender-specific, it's a paradigm that can corrupt anyone, at any age, from almost any culture.

More and more statistics are coming out showing more men who are heart-led and working for gender equality (which makes them Feminists). With strong spines of direction and ambition, and with profoundly tender attentiveness, these men are embodying wholeness. We are all going to reap the rewards of that brave love.

Divinely Feminine is not about being in a goddess dancing circle or being super orgasmic. (Because you can do/be all of those things and get way out of balance.) And the Divine Feminine sure ain't about being the first female president, dean, or CEO of anything. Ranking high in a broken system doesn't necessarily make you a heroine of feminism thou it well could, and women's history is abundant with those true pioneers.

The Divine Feminine is about balance. It's the merge of The Great Father and The Great Mother within us all and that divine union then expresses itself using a feminine-energy vehicle upholding and emphasizing it's qualities.

First the merge of the masculine and the feminine has to happen, for the truly Divine Feminine to come into form and then that wholeness expresses itself in predominately womanly ways. Feminine + masculine union gets communicated in the language of "feminine". (OR... if you identify as a guy devoted to wholeness, then it's Feminine + masculine union being communicated in the language of "masculine".) Two ideas merge, and then they express themselves in a specific way.

The Divine Feminine is the warrior and the healer in one package. The Divine Feminine is justice and mercy carried out with grace. It's economics and the arts that nurtures the entire world.

We are direct and we hunt for opportunities, these are mostly masculine qualities. We are deeply intuitive and nurturing these are mostly feminine qualities. We are at our best when we express all of these qualities which means we are compassionate often softly spoken and our business operates on a triple bottom line. We want everyone to be well fed even if that means we have to share our own food, that's when we are living the Divine Feminine.

The fundamentals of Balance throughout the universe are two equal and opposite forces play tag and in their interaction all things are created. Those that move towards balance evolve, while those that move towards inbalance devolve. The Feminine isn't a lady label that you see with your eyes, it's a way of being that can only be seen with the intelligence of the heart.

# CHAPTER 2

# THE ALCHEMICAL YOU

If you bring forth what is within you, what you bring forth will save you. If you do not bring forth what is within you, what you do not bring forth will destroy you.

Alchemy pertains to the process of transmuting base metals to silver or gold. The search for the 'gold' in each person is the fundamental focus. Alchemy represents the circular process of individuation, in which internal opposits conflicts, and the conscious and unconscious is assimilated and integrated to become the journey towards wholeness.

We begin at the seed level with our prime material, or primary substance. It is our original material from whence we came, and it is paradoxically where we both begin and end our process of individuality. Alchemy seeks to transmute ordinary consciousness into cosmic consiousness and back to personal consciousness. It teaches that there is a power greater than yourself and you are a part of it. "There is no rebirth of consciousness without pain".

A wall must be hit a wall of non success in order for a harsh awakening to occur which prompts great psychological change and opens us up to inner exploration. Sometimes this opening allows grace and brings enlightenment or sometimes Karma is balanced and enlightenment comes.

However, when this happens there must be a willingness to let go and let God as they say. We can venture into the realm of facing our sources of oppression, and the illusions, fears, emotions and defenses that prevent that fragile ego from being crushed.

The ego is now ready to attach to the abstract plane beyond the sensory world. One's solid sense of identity is raised to a higher level and the Spirit hidden in matter reveals itself. We are ready to transcend the self and our quest for meaning takes on more far-reaching implications. Dualistic thinking kept us separate and polarized.

As we travel our journey of individuality our sense of self becomes less contaminated by projection and we move closer towards our essence. The hero/heroine continues to face the darkness and willingly allows fantasy and illusion to die. With a new consciousness of who we are.

Here we venture into the watery realm of the unconscious. Dream analysis, meditation, creative expression, and immersion in the world of imagination and fantasy characterize this process. The primal energy of the unconscious helps to dissolve rigidity and judgment. We become more fluid and cleansed. We become more real.

With a new consciousness of who we are, we can choose what we need to release so as to allow one's true nature to fully emerge. This sorting though, or separating our true essence from superfluous outmoded ways of being, fosters the ability to temper the tenacious need for security. We risk revealing ourselves with all our beautiful defects and strengths.

Emotions which can be the most harmful to our mind and bodies create fear and anger. All negative emotions of fear, anger, hostility, jealousy, greed will effect he or she that feels them. This is very hard to to overcome but if one is to have a long life one must harbour unconditional love.

# CHAPTER 3

# STORIES OF THE FEMININE DIVINE

The concept of the Feminine Divine has taken on form and, like an avalanche is sweeping through humanity. People will grasp the creational knowledge given to us in the great work of religion to explain a concept, which has been linked to the many tales of the past.

> **1.** In the beginning, God created the heavens and the earth. The Heavens are known to the human race as the Divine realm. Since

God created the Divine, it means that God is not Divine but something higher, for in truth, God is not Divine. The gulf between God and the Divine realm seems so great that not even the human spirit can begin to conceptualize the distance involved. Everything outside of God can be pictured as the radiations of God and between the Divine realm and God lies an inconceivably ocean of flames without the possibility of taking on form.

Within this flame a female took on form which is the will of God and the love of God. These forms, though separate from each other and therefore personal, were united by a delicate ware of form which also becomes personal in the most delicate beauty of feminine essence.

Quite apart from that, surrounding these forms, countless executive beings took on forms. These included, as the foremost, the seven Archangels of which Lucifer was one. The female being through which these forms takes place has her figure transgressing whole worlds so to say, and at her footstool stands the garden of all virtues. In charge of this garden is an executive being in change of purity for womanhood, later to be known in creation as the Feminine Divine.

> **2.** In the beginning, God created the Divine, and later beneath, the creations came into being. This was referred to as the earth in the Genesis creation story. Creation actually started with the first words "Let there be Light", which brought out light to the dark formless void, and then with the traveling of the light radiation that shot out, the creations were formed, first the seven planes of the highest spiritual and then the next seven planes of the spiritual.
>
> Hence the inhabitants of the seven higher planes, at the end of the seventh plane, were the ones that came together and said "Let us create man in our own image". So the human

spiritual was created after the likeness of the primordial beings. This comprise of the physical world, the three astral planes and there planes of ether. The imperfection of these creations saddened them, and a voice thundered from above: "wait for the promised one who will put things right". This was rendered correctly in the Holy Grail legends with the promise of the coming of the one.

**3.** Unconscious spirit germs in paradise have to leave paradise to the worlds of matter where, as lords in the worlds of matter, they can mature and get back to paradise where they belong forever. The story of these journey and activities are given to us by Jesus in the parable of the prodigal son.

**4.** One of the Archangels, Lucifer, was sent down to help the fledgling human spirits in the world of matter. Instead of helping them in love, he introduced the principle of temptation to condemn and destruction the weak ones. This brought about his being cut off from his origin thereby becoming the strongest spirit in the world of matter. His colleagues in the Divine wept hot tears and the tears fell on him but he had become even too insensitive to feel it.

**5.** Divine feminine pleaded to be allowed to help the womanhood on earth because if woman on earth could change, Mankind will generally change. It was granted, and she was allowed to descend with the king of the Holy Grail where she was to incarnate on earth first to acquaint herself with the world of matter before the time of the sacred mission. It was then she was allowed to raise the chalice for the first time to hand it to the one.

**6.** Divine Feminine was incarnated in Egypt at that time where Mary Magdalene was her earthly mother. Hence Mary Magdalene's involvement with the Divine Feminine was that she was once her mother on earth before she was later incarnated in the tiny Island of Magdalla where she grew up, together with Mary of Bethany, to become one of the female disciples of Christ. Here so much has been woven around the personality of Mary Magdalene that does not come near to conforming to the truth.

**7.** At the same period that the Divine Feminine lived as a child in Egypt of Iran but was born to the prince of Iran but was brought up some where else, he later founded a kingdom in Sudan where he took the Divine Feminine into his custody, together with her mother and later Juricheo, the foster mother of Moses. He walked closely with Moses from his Kingdom, Is-ra. Moses was later to liberate his people of Is-ra-el from the bondage of Egypt.

It is the activities of the God-man, his efforts to acquaint himself with his creations, and the attempt by the darkness led by Lucifer to smoother his works that was actually depicted in revelations chapter 12.

The first woman to take on form in the vicinity of the proximity of God was the woman, the God-man is the child and Lucifer was the dragon. His activities on earths during the time of Moses was depicted as the birth of the child.

He was actually assassinated by the Egyptian Pharaoh Ramses II, and the Divine Feminine left with him. It took two times and half a time for him to come back to earth - three thousand five hundred years from the time of Moses of this time of his knowledge of creation and/of the world judgment. He still came with the Divine Feminine.

# Divine feminine:
# Bringing back the essence

Though the divine feminine archetypes were accepted and venerated from the ancient days of human civilizations, somewhere down the line this strong feminine connection was discarded in many of the modern religions. Today we are paying the price for that mistake. Most of the problems that are seen in today's world are the result of looking at the supreme as "He" and this "He" is attributed with the bloodshed of holy wars and conquests. The reality is far away from this myopic view. The supreme force in actuality is the culmination of the feminine and masculine principles of nature in a universal void which is devoid of any beginning or end. This is reality and the ultimate truth of life which clearly reveals to us that the feminine principle is the source of birth, nurturing, creative and generative change as well as the reason for decay, death and regeneration.

# Divine feminine:
# The manifestation of the feminine principle

Unless we accept the manifestation of the feminine principle or divine feminine in the form of birth, growth, death, decay, transformation and rebirth, we would not be able to appreciate the working of the universe. In fact the divine feminine or the feminine principle is responsible for the nurturing and sustaining influence of the universe and it is the absolute source for the proactive and initiating nature of the masculine. This is true within us as well as the external universe. Further we need to understand that it is only the interplay of the feminine and masculine that is responsible for the genesis of creativity and here once again let me reemphasize on the fact that the masculine exsist because of the feminine and if we don't have the feminine as the source then we don't have any action based on the masculine.

# The divine feminine:
# The interplay of the feminine and masculine principles

In Hinduism it is very clearly taught that all creativity in this universe is the result of the interplay of the divine feminine and masculine. There is truth in the symbolism of Yin/Yang where the black and white forces interact to create the universe. Tibetan Buddhist respect this interplay of the divine feminine and masculine through the symbolization of the dorge and the bell. The Bell is the feminine and the dorge the masculine aspect. All rituals are done with the help of these symbols. We must understand the fact that the truth is to see the universe as a whole and not separate he or she or the dark or the light or the day or night. The universe is in fact the interplay of all these manifestations. Further there is no question of any existence of the masculine without the existence of the feminine principle. The feminine principle is the beginning, the present and the end of everything and the masculine is just an attribute supporting this universal phenomenon.

## Divine feminine:
## It exists within all of us

The irony of today's world is that we only see one half of the truth which is the secondary and dependent half. We have in fact become blind to the primary and independent aspect of the truth. As a result of this anomaly and its consequence in the form of uncontrolled manifestation of the masculine principle, we can see great imbalance in the universe.

All the chaos and destruction that we are seeing today is the result of this anomaly and imbalance.

To restore the balance of the universe we need to rekindle the divine feminine that actually exists in all of us. That which exists within us has to be called upon and expressed within our own inner self as well as the external universe.

Only this energy can propel us towards the true direction and purpose of our life. The Mantra is to achieve a balance in life by evoking the feminine and move towards the path of ultimate liberation. Once we start achieving the balance within our own inner self, then it starts manifesting in our relationships with others and the world at large. This is the only way to bring back the balance in the universe.

# CHAPTER 4

# WHOLE BRAIN THINKING

For thousands of years we have looked out to the heavens or inside ourselves to contemplate God's nature. In the process of seeking into a vast emptiness we have forgotten about the sacred power of the present moment which is creatively happening through us and in the world around us. It is time for us all to move beyond culture's left brain focus on a disembodied and transcendent God, a focus which has split apart spirit and matter. It is time to bring back the fullness of all that exists.

In Western cultures women and men are taught to live in their minds (left brain) and to doubt their own intuitive and instinctive knowledge (right brain). By primarily valuing the left brain hemisphere, we become disconnected from our bodies and from nature and we limit our potential creativity and our intellectual flexibility to fully experience and understand our lives and the world.

## Whole Brain Thinking - Honoring the Divine Feminine

How can we understand and experience the nature of God in the Divine Feminine aspects of fullness and love while still honoring Divine Masculine aspects of emptiness and freedom? We can begin by becoming more consciously aware in daily life. Then, as we mature and evolve in skill and wisdom, we will learn to connect with the eternal, cosmic mind of God. Most will find that they have reversed this process because of our culture's predominate focus on a distant God who dwells in Heaven. Either path still leads to the One so that the essential task is to combine and then integrate the two aspects of God to form one whole, non-dual perspective.

## What is Whole Braining Thinking?

Whole brain thinking is the ability to use both the left and the right brain adeptly. The corpus callosum facilitates this connection - a large band of neural fibers that connects the two cerebral hemispheres. This connecting band of tissue in women is thicker than in men, raising the question, *"How is a woman's way of experiencing God going to be influenced by this thicker bridge between the two hemispheres?"*

Because women have an enhanced ability to use both left and right brain hemispheres, women have the most to offer in healing the split between the masculine way of understanding

God (emptiness and freedom) with the feminine way of understanding God (fullness, love and the present moment).

## What is the Divine Feminine Way to God?

The feminine is the core of creation that is love. Creation, love and the Divine Feminine are one and the same. Every woman instinctively knows that she is at the center of this great creative mystery that is unfolding in the moment. The Divine Feminine aspects of God put us in touch with our own bodies, our own imagery and our own truth and in so doing we awaken to what is meaningful in our lives. She values all things as important to the health of the whole and recognizes our mutual connectedness. Her fearless embrace of feeling in the present moment can remind us of the incredible mystery and sacred power of life.

*"Non-dual realization embraces both emptiness (masculine) and matter/form (feminine) aspects. "Being" and "becoming" are both parts of a non-dual, self realization.»*

## What Does the Divine Feminine Value?

The Divine Feminine values all matter - living beings and nonliving natural objects and also every part of all things - as important to the health of the whole. She recognizes our mutual interdependence and connectedness to all things for survival, well-being and evolutionary vibrancy. She places a great deal of significance on having good relationships based on mutual cooperation and she uses intuitive, instinctive knowledge.

## Moving Into Whole Brain Thinking

When women and men remember what the Divine Feminine really values, we realize we must include all perspectives to gain an understanding of the wholeness and connectedness of life. To do so we must dive fearlessly into the mystery of the pain and suffering that is part of the great feminine initiation into the cycles of creation.

We honor the Great Mother Goddess when we embrace life as it is. She embodies the wisdom of forgiveness and turns us to what is hidden in darkness to be reborn in a powerful new way. We can then focus on the present moment where anything is possible and no separation exists if we listen to and respond courageously to our intuitive wisdom.

With greater understanding of the differences between right and left brain thinking and appreciation of what the divine feminine values, we have the opportunity to return to the beneficial wholeness of both the masculine (ascending) and feminine (descending) aspects of God united in oneness.

Integrating Divine Feminine and Masculine Principles Into Your Life Reawakening to the divine feminine is a union of embodying her principles in our daily lives as well as intellectually integrating and including the bright light of masculine consciousness. We combine these two by:

> **1.** Enjoying the world with our five senses while using our sixth sense - intuitive knowledge. Intuitive knowledge makes something known by focusing our attention on universal knowledge or collective consciousness.
>
> **2.** Seeing the parts then integrating and combining them to form a whole. Western cultures teach the scientific method of separating the parts from the whole and calling them truth. As we broaden

our knowledge, we learn that just because something looks true, doesn't mean it's the only truth or absolute truth.

**3.** Being and Becoming - learning to meditate, pray or contemplate while staying in present time, in our bodies, for our own needs as well as the moment's.

**4.** Traveling deeply into space to experience emptiness, oneness and freedom and then returning and going deeply into the cycles and mystery of creation in order to become empowered and reborn in a new way. We can master ascending (masculine way to God) and descending (feminine way to God) at the same time.

Exercises for Becoming More Whole Brained People use to say if you were logical, you were definitely left-brained, and if you were creative, you were definitely right-brained.

This is no longer the case. New research indicates that there's more flexibility in our brains and we can train our brains to become more organized, creative or better able to process all sorts of information. Knowing where our strengths and weaknesses are can help us strengthen the weaker hemisphere. Here are some ways to strengthen the left or right hemispheres:

**Left Brain Exercises**

**1. Make lists**

One method of getting into details is to outline what must be done. Bite sized chunks of daily tasks are an excellent way to engage the left hemisphere and also to overcome apparently impossible hurdles.

**2. Pay attentions to details**

The left hemisphere is about details and linear thinking. Notice the details in the surrounding environment and connect to what is happening through the power of observation.

**3. Change your immediate environment**

Changing surroundings is an opportunity to change thinking because the mind will not have its familiar environment to cue it into old habits. Create an environment that has beautiful, calming, and enjoyable details.

## Right Brain Exercises

### 1. Keep the bigger picture in mind

Take time to become aware of the greater scheme of life and larger reoccurring patterns.

### 2. Creative visualization

Learn to quit the chatter in the mind and to allow the spatial, holistic and much more unconscious right brain do its work. Meditation and contemplative practices are useful techniques to quit the left brain.

### 3. Practice spatial rotation exercises

The right brain is involved in spatial tasks as well as holistic vision. Imagine objects rotating in space. Keep a clear image of the object while it is moving.

## 4. Learn to trust intuitive information

Allow the right brain the opportunity to function by reflecting on unique and creative thoughts. Honor the insights received through day dreams, visions and imaginings. Relax and enjoy their creative possibilities.

# CHAPTER 5

# THE RETURN OF THE FEMININE

Visionaries, luminaries, modern mystics along with more practical thought leaders found in every field including, economists, business people and environmentalists, as well as everyday people, have made a claim that 2017 is the year of this paradigm shift. This new energy is the return of the Divine Soul's Feminine Energy.

We are in just the beginning of a long new cycle of a new vibration alignment in which everything including our very essence, our souls is in a huge awakening time. While this is exciting news, it is also transitional and that is often unsettling as the balance that once was is no longer and a new normal is being formed. It will take a very long time to see the overall results but everyday when we act in courage we are co-creating this new normal. The over all shift is from the patriarch to equality between it and the matriarch. The new vibration, involves the divine soul's fememine energy flow. What is the Divine Soul's Feminine energy?

The energy of the Divine Feminine is a unique and natural experience.. Unique in that the feminine energy is present in anything or anyone, including men when they are nourishing and sustaining life. The feminine energy is automatically plugged into being connected to others. Women as holders of that energy hold a genuine authentic capacity of empathy for one another's a challenges, and to encourage and nurture each others hidden potential. Life is sustainable when this happens.

It is what the feminine energy does so well. It sustains and fills our empty buckets with the kind of juice and zest we need to carry on and carry out our desires. Everything that is life affirming and sustaining is the Divine Feminine Energy. Carrying and facilitating this energy is the highest value of women's work during her lifetime. With its help we can activate a new age of human possibilities and potential for ways of being that we haven't even dreamt yet.

We are in the midst of the shift from the ego to the essence of ourselves; our soul's awakening and participating in our daily lives in bigger ways. It is the soul over matter and heart over the head mindset-shift that demands new tools and training so we can become aligned to these shifts and changes. It's either, evolve or we as a species may die.

Humanity is being taken to the point where it will have to choose between suicide and adoration. It will be a breaking point in having to set a new course in our economic, political and environmental but most importantly we as individuals have to step into our greatest fears our own brilliance and do those things that we are feeling the urge to do.

This is a unique time in history in which the balance of our very planet is awakening to make the shift to the Divine Soul's feminine flow to sustain and learn to live from our heart and soul. Make the decision to cross over the threshold into personal transformation and personal healing so that your gifts can claim a stake in a new space.

You are an important piece of the larger picture. New ways of relating to one another on this planet are being birthed as we surrender and align to the energy of the Divine Soul's Feminine flow. Each of us can become powerful change.

**How can you begin to implement the divine energy of the feminine in your life?**

## DIVINE FEMININE

Call in the divine feminine energy into your lives by asking the miracle, the magic, and the mystery to be a part of your daily life and for your business.

Remove isolation. Sure it is okay to allow yourself time to work through a sticky point but after 3 days, reach out and get help. Asking for help is the way the divine feminine can come through your friend or mentor and give you just the boost what you need to get back on track.

# CHAPTER 6

# FEMININE POWER

At a party, you see a woman or man across the room with a charisma that is out of this world. On the street, you notice a woman or man walking towards you with a stride that leaves you in awe. At work, you watch the new sales manager address everyone with such finesse and ease that you feel envy creeping up your spine. At a restaurant, your eye catches a voluptuous vixen flirting with the waiter with such ease and it leaves you wondering, how does he or she do that? What do all of these people have in common?

They possess the power of the feminine. This type of Mystical Radiance permeates and radiates from people who are anchored within their body. Their energy speaks volumes and they need not say a word.

These people have no need to be loud, to display or solicit attention from others. Their power is not dependent on outside forces; they have developed their inner forces to feed, nourish and serve them. They rely on inner resources for counsel, guidance and directives. They have lifted the veils of delusional feminine ideology and integrated the essence of authentic feminine energy. These people did not arrive to such a destination without peril. They struggled, wept, despaired and rose from the ashes like a phoenix.

Feminine power in the 21st century is still misunderstood, often times by women themselves. I have witnessed women behave in such inappropriate ways when it came to beauty, men, money and popularity. It is as if on a subliminal level of the feminine soul has been convinced that the bread crumbs tossed her way could satisfy her immense nature.

Lack of personal power is a learned behavior. Some of us learn from our parents, grandparents or other relatives who populate our family tree. We absorb subliminal messages from them to settle for less in the realm of money, career, and relationships.

In subliminal ways, we are encouraged to stay just like them. However, each generation is destined to break free from such limitations and begin the journey to self-realization. It is a monumental task but one worth undertaking.

Certain religions and societies around the world expect nothing more from a woman than her ability to bear children. In this societal or religious group, a woman can only fulfill her biological destiny and nothing more. She will not be allowed to develop her Divine Feminine potential.

Instead, she will be encouraged to give her power away and compromise her identity in the process.

In society, women are taught from a young age to grow up and be the perfect woman. They are expected to do it all and if they can't do it all, there is something wrong. Theye are taught that everything in the world is limited - finances, jobs, men, love, promotions, etc. They are told that sex is the only weapon they have to ensure they get what they want.

They are told self-sacrifice is a noble act. They are told that a woman's worth depends on who she marries, where she lives, the size of the rock on her finger, the children she bears, the car she drives, where she shops, the champagne she drinks, and of course, her dress size.

Society has devised so many distractions for the modern woman to keep her from owning her power. Women are expected to hide their intelligence, their power and their strength in order to remain in good favor with the men in their lives. Being influenced by these voices and believing them limits a woman's sense of individuality. So many try to live by these standards only to discover the monster of discontentment is lurking just beneath the surface. The modern woman lives in a time where her possibilities are endless and her potential ripe. All this freedom has not contributed to her happiness but has been the cause of her confusion.

The feminine face of God has enough influence to veto the patriarchal brand of power. However, rarely has this been the case. Women through the centuries were taught to solicit affections from man but to care nothing about his integrity or moral character. They allowed his unsavory conduct and failed to hold him accountable. The ancient sisters were not in a position to draw the line but now they are.

For every woman who holds the people in her life accountable teaches them to be mindful in the future of thought, word and deed. Every time a woman says 'This is unacceptable' to her lovers, friends and family, she helps to straighten out the fabric of her being and that of the collective.

Also, Women need to reclaim being treated like ladies and learn to walk away when it's otherwise. Women need to develop, what I call, emotional backbone. When you have emotional backbone, you no longer operate on fear but fearlessness. if you speak your truth you know your chronic headaches will disappear.

Women must learn to rely on the higher self for all the things they currently want from others.

This draws people to you not because the energy you exude piques curiosity or makes people feel amazing in your presence. They can't get enough of you and remember you haven't even done anything. You are simply being your higher self. Just being you is enough to receive, warm smiles and flattering compliments without the need to be outrageous or to hide your magnificence. A word to the wise, seek out self-realized women and men try to learn from them. They have been in your shoes, they have struggled with the questions and their lives mirror the answers. They know the terrain by heart and can guide your footsteps.

# CHAPTER 7

# SURRENDERING TO DIVINE FEMININE

One of the greatest opportunities and challenges for men or women in this day and age is surrendering to the Divine Feminine. The current state of humanity as a civilization and the world we live in is a reflection of the collective consciousness that has been dominant for thousands of years.

One particular aspect of this collective consciousness has been the distorted and domineering aspect of the masculine energy within society. The polar opposite effect of the dominant masculine energy has been the repression of the feminine energy both within ourselves and through the outer manifestations of reality.

Nothing has been more devastating towards the evolution and ascension of humanity to a higher state of consciousness based on love, cooperation and oneness than the Masculine-Feminine Rift. And the only way to transcend and heal this evolutionary impediment is for humanity to experience the surrendering to the Divine Feminine. This surrender can only occur within ourselves and requires more than a shift of belief systems and ways of thinking, it requires a re-patterning of our DNA.

Let's first start by describing some of the energy signatures or qualities of masculine and feminine energies:

| **Masculine Energy** | **Feminine Energy** |
|---|---|
| Action | Presence |
| Control and Righteousness | Surrender |
| Manifested Matter | Unmanifested Matter (Void/Source) |
| Competition | Cooperation/Support |
| Provider | Nurture |
| Rational | Intuition/Emotional Intelligence |

Whether you are a man or a woman, you have ALL of these energies within you, yet your gender will greatly determine which energies will tend to be expressed more through your physiology (brain, hormones, body figure, voice tonality), emotions, mental constructions and soul vibration.

Despite having all these energies within, most of humanity has revolved for some time now around in what appears to be a masculine energy dominant world where outer success and worldly achievements are valued more than intuition, where emotional expression equals weakness, where the greatness of motherhood has been diminished and where competition, greed for power and the need for control have taken over the joy and grace of life/existence itself.

The first step to balance these inner masculine and feminine energies is to release the Pride and or Ego. There is nothing wrong with a feeling of pride for having done a good job, etc. but when you live for your pride, that's when it can become a problem. When you are constantly fueling the ego, it is like chasing an illusive dragon or trying to quench an unending thirst.

The ego must constantly be filled with pride to make the host feel okay. However, there is nothing wrong with the host feeling okay. The difference is in the motivation. Living for pride alone is an addiction of sorts that stems from a place that feels less than or un-whole, in my personal layperson's perspective.

If one is seeking the ego feed of pride alone to feel good, know that the action will only ever result in a short-lived high of sorts. However, other pursuits from a more healthy place will have longer lasting results - like being kind to self and others just for the opportunity itself to be kind. That feels good but to take too much pride in that and to hold yourself above others in that is where the motivation comes into focus.

So, I would say that you don't need to ditch your pride but just don't let it stand between you and what is most beautiful and magical in life. This is exactly what I am doing with this e-book it will assist people to embody their Higher Self and heal the Male-Female Rift (this healing session is available to everyone). This is the most important and crucial step to take for any person who desire to balance their inner masculine and feminine energies and experience a re-birth in consciousness. Once this step is taken the next step consists in expressing that inner balance through your outer reality.

In my own relationship my dominant masculine energies and the repressed feminine energies manifested mainly through the need to be right, the need to control and repressing my emotions. Therefore my Higher Self guided me to make a conscious decision and develop new ways of being where I:

- Drop my sense of self-righteousness and the need to control everything
- Honor her voice and opinions
- Honor her emotions and hold a safe space for her to express them
- Honor my own emotions and express them in functional and healthy ways

These conscious actions have resulted in greater intuition, enhanced emotional intelligence, greater sense of compassion, becoming more empathic, enhanced energy healing abilities, greater state of presence and deepening the states of allowing.

When it comes to women, some have repressed their Divine Feminine energies in order to exalt their masculine energies in hopes to survive in this male dominated world. The women who consciously, subconsciously or unconsciously choose to repress their feminine energies will often adopt the masculine traits of competition, control and the need for external power.

What do you think happens when a woman who has repressed her feminine energies and now has overactive masculine energies gets into a relationship with a man who has a dominant masculine energy? Fights, arguments and power struggles will manifest constantly in the relationship.

So when the man is able to surrender to the Divine Feminine and the woman surrenders to the Divine Masculine, the woman can drop the need to control everything, including sex, and the male finally can relax and drop the whole facade to try to impress her with success, money and power.

The ultimate result is a relationship where both partners can hold and own their corresponding balanced ratio of masculine and feminine energies, creating a magnetic attraction and celebration of their own uniqueness and differences.

www.ingramcontent.com/pod-product-compliance
Lightning Source LLC
Chambersburg PA
CBHW052118070526
44584CB00017B/2544